HACKNEY HOUSES

A guide to
improvement
conservation
maintenance

A Hackney Society Publication

FOREWORD

This book is an initiative of the Hackney Society with financial assistance from the London Borough of Hackney through the Inner City Partnership Programme. Although the views expressed are those of the Society and not of the Council I am happy to recommend it because the aim of improving the Borough is shared both by the Council and particularly by the officers of the Planning Department. I hope this book will help you to improve your house and all of us to improve the Borough.

Richard Gee
Vice-Chairman
Planning Committee
1982

Author: Helen Peacock
Photos: Mark Pilkington
         Clemens Deilmann
Illustration: Marilyn Day
Layout: Mark Pilkington
        Helen Peacock

With assistance from:

The Hackney Society
Patrick Hammill
Michael Hunter

The Planning Division of the
London Borough of Hackney
Mike New, Angela Norris,
David French

Second Edition 1987
© The Hackney Society

INTRODUCTION

'Hackney Houses' was first published in 1982. This edition is a reprint with only minor revisions to ensure that the information section shows current addresses. However if the book is the same as before the housing market has changed dramatically in the last six years, both in terms of the value of property, and in the considerable involvement of housing developers in addition to house owners.

Although wholesale redevelopment and the tower block are no longer altering Hackney in the way they did, Hackney is still changing. One of the most significant changes could be as the people living in the Borough maintain and improve their houses.

The purpose of the book remains the same, to remind people that the character of Hackney is made up of many individual houses, and the neighbourhoods that they form. Each house or street has its own character and if modernised without thought this can easily be destroyed.

This is not a do-it-yourself manual, nor is it a history book, though it does say something about the historical background of Hackney's houses. It suggests that there are ways of altering a house which contribute to the street rather than harm it. Not everyone may agree with the opinions expressed but it is hoped that this book will help you to decide, for what happens to the ordinary houses of Hackney is just as important in shaping the Borough as what happens to its well known historic buildings.

CONTENTS

GROWTH AND CHANGE

In 1800 Hackney consisted of fields, country estates, and villages. As London expanded the fields and estates were gradually built on until those villages of Dalston, Shacklewell Homerton, Stoke Newington, Upper and Lower Clapton, and Hackney joined together to form a new suburb of the city. In 1801 approximately 50,000 people lived in the area we now call Hackney, by 1851 it had risen to approx. 170,000, and to 370,000 in 1901.

It was to house this growing population that the houses we see today were built. Londoners sold their fields and estates for development. Houses were built for sale or for rent to the professional classes, business-men, and their clerks; as well as their own servants, the shopkeepers, and others who served them less directly. By 1900 Hackney was becoming less fashionable, the better off moved further out to the suburbs, and new and often poorer people moved into the rented accommodation that was vacated. The rack renting landlord became a characteristic figure, and spent as little as possible on their property. By the 2nd World War much of the housing was poorly maintained and lacking in modern amenities, far below the standards of the housing estates being built further out of London in places like Dagenham.

Post-War Housing.

Hitlers bombs brought this slow decay to a climax for many streets and necessitated large scale re-building. There was also a widespread hope after the war to build a new life in a new environment. To the politicians, architects and planners of the time, many of the streets that were left appeared old and insanitary. Many felt that there was an opportunity to build a new city, and politicians spoke of sweeping demolition and re-development. Their vision was sincere though it was an ideal which has failed to provide the new communities that were hoped for. The old Borough of Shoreditch began a rolling programme of re-development, the necessity of rebuilding war damage was compounded by a vision of a new world: indeed it is said that more houses were destroyed by the bull-dozer than by the bombs. In the Boroughs of Hackney and Stoke Newington it was only later, when the Boroughs were amalgamated, that such policies became general, and a rolling programme of re-development laid down for the whole borough up to 1975. Encouraged by governments that gave high subsidies for tower blocks and little for improvement, numerous streets of sound houses that had formed communities were demolished. More-over apart from the demolition, the grand plans themselves did much harm in blighting the houses left standing.

High-Rise in Hackney

In the early sixties the wastefulness of such redevelopment was increasingly apparent and pressure grew for a change; by 1969 central government responded, ahead of many local authorities, and money was made available for improvement areas. In 1970, Hackney declared 2 general improvement areas, the first Borough in London to do so, and there were signs that the policy was moving from redevelopment to rehabilitation. This initiative was, however, short-lived; control of the Borough changed at the next election and whilst arguments over policy were fought out within the council so blight and redevelopment continued, and improvement of existing houses remained an opportunity largely ignored by Hackney Council.

Initiative for change came from local people, for many in the Borough were questioning the Council's policies both because of the indiscriminate way in which good houses were demolished together with the bad, and because the problems of living on the new estates were becoming sadly apparent.

Public concern forced the Council to attempt to justify its plans at Public Enquiries such as Sanford Terrace, where permission to demolish a Georgian Terrace was refused; the Ferncliff Road Enquiry where permission to demolish a terrace of listed buildings was refused, and Mapledene, where redevelopment plans were refused. Sanford Terrace was, later renovated by the Council. Through these, and other, particular cases, increasing government pressure, and increasing general interest to retain familiar streets and their houses, so Council policy changed.

Today the original houses of Hackney are still having to change, as existing owners and tenants, and new owners moving into the Borough, modernise their homes, and alter the

Mapledene where redevelopment plans were turned down.

familiar houses and streets.

Since the 1950s and up until the present day many of the owner occupiers of Hackney have been gripped by the various changing fashions and fads of so-called 'modernisation'. The 50s and 60s saw people smashing out the fronts of their houses to put in picture windows in a vain attempt to make the compact and characterful Victorian house into a modern streamlined machine. Since then there have been mock Georgian doors, windows and lamps, glass doors, aluminium windows, in fact anything and everything that is part of the desire to make the Victorian house into what it is not and pretend that it is something else.

The rehabilitation of older houses is not an easy task. Many people, confronted with this problem, took the line of minimum resistance and had little thought for the repercussions of badly conceived and badly built alterations. The problems that they confronted, and are still confronting today, are by no means small and the persuasive literature of the building trade, the Do-it-yourself bonanza which made everything seem easy and the high cost of using an architect have all contributed towards this insensitive approach to rehabilitation.

Changing views about the value of 19th century houses are leading towards the rejection of alterations

that destroy their character. Taste now recognises that the original building and its construction has a beauty of its own. Rehabilitation work is a part of any respectable council's programmes and many individuals are putting time and money into sensible and sensitive improvement of their houses. Unfortunately, whether council owned or privately owned, the amount of money available in grants is not sufficient to do justice to the years of neglect or blight.

Economic and political conditions make it increasingly unlikely that large areas of Hackney will be redeveloped in the immediate future. Although major battles have been won, they could still be lost if neglect and decay destroy the houses that were once threatened by demolition. Conservation is still an issue that needs fighting for.

DECAY

The aftermath of Hackney's recent history is still with us. The consequences of neglect and planning blight has led to considerable decay

The reasons why some areas of cities decay, while others do not, are related to much wider issues than simply the actions of individuals and how they treat their own houses. The city planning aspects such as transport provision, new road building, location of industry and employment, etc. the way local authorities allocate money, the priorities they have and the interrelationship of these factors with building societies and banks who lend money all play a part in how and why parts of cities decay. Decay occurs through lack of investment but why there is lack of investment is a complicated economic, political and social issue. One aspect is, however, clear. Those areas which have forceful, vociferous and influential groups working in them are less likely to suffer decay.

The physical decay of individual houses, of streets and of whole areas has a direct effect on the spirit of the communities that live in cities. Decay leads people to lose respect for their surroundings, encourages vandalism, and is not only depressing for those who live in decaying streets but for those who pass through them.

Sensible house maintenance will last a long time, save money and look good. Neglecting essential repairs can lead to the need to do expensive work at a later date. If a roof has been left until it reaches a state of considerable decay then the slates and timbers may need to be extensively renewed. This fact is only common sense as is most of the battle against decay in buildings.

One house that brightly and self-confidently shows itself well maintained in a street of neglected houses is something that is immediately noticed. At the same time a house that is neglected can detract from the visual quality of the whole street. A number of decaying houses in an area can seriously take away from the overall character and quality of the area.

Of course the problem of neglect is not always in the hands of home owners; areas of Local Authority and Greater London Council owned property have in the past been left empty and allowed to decay. This kind of unforgivable neglect still goes on today, and, in the end, it may be this kind of negligence that destroys Hackney. All of us have the responsibility to be aware of what is happening to our heritage and to protest strongly.

The photographs on this page show some of the decay that can be found in many areas of Hackney. The following pages show some areas that, despite recent history and despite the decay in other parts of the Borough, have managed to keep the character that they were intended to have.

Each of the areas chosen represents some aspect of Hackney; for example houses next to parks, local shopping areas, etc. The areas are distributed throughout the Borough as can be seen from the map at the end of the book.

UNIFORMITY WITHOUT MONOTONY

Clapton Pond

The repeated house types of these early Edwardian houses, with two storey terraces lining regular streets, are pleasant because of their completeness. By and large, people have kept their homes in good order and respected the original details of these solidly built houses.

At first glance, each street appears the same, but, on closer inspection it can be seen that within the apparent uniformity there are different roofs, different details around doors and windows as well as the note of individuality that each owner gives to the house.

Tree lined Fletching Road has interesting variety of roof level and pleasant details around doors and windows.

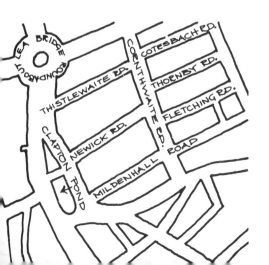

Houses in the same area with simpler rooves and plasterwork arches over doorways.

Shacklewell Green

These few streets behind Shacklewell Green make a small composition of late Victorian 'artisan' houses of the 1880s. The shops facing the green are part of the regular rythmn and a few of the original shop front details are intact. The houses themselves are plain, by Victorian standards, but brick arches over the doors, date plaques and other decorative plaques with moulded fruits and flowers give individuality to the repeated house types.

Perch Street curving round to meet Seal Street.

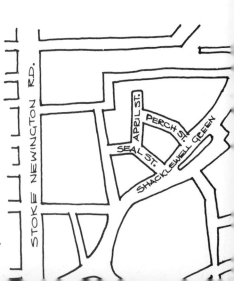

Three storey corner houses (on both sides of Perch Street) face on to Shacklewell Green. The detail work is slightly more ornate.

11

VICTORIAN SPLENDOUR

Middleton Road shown with a backdrop of the 20th century answer to the housing problem.

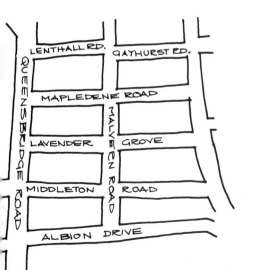

Mapledene

This area of houses from the 1850s shows considerable variety with semi-detached houses, continuous terraces of 2 storey houses and 3 storey terraces as well. Nevertheless, certain elements bind it together as an area despite some demolition and recent rebuilding nearby. Many original windows and doors remain and the fine brickwork of the houses has stood the test of time. The detailed work tends to be more austere and classical than the later Victorian flamboyance.

Bethune Road Area

To the north of the Borough, this area contains some buildings listed as of historic importance, notably the Allens Estate of 1873 (in Bethune Road itself). Nearby there are many interesting houses of varied types that knit together with the regular pattern of streets. A great variety of different details can be found from semi-colour brick arches to classical columns, iron railings and house name plaques.

Houses in St. Kildas Road with ornate plaster work details around doors and windows. Each house has small variations in the detail work.

House in Bethune Road showing the grander style of these large Victorian houses. Careful detailing of bands of plasterwork binds the different storey heights together.

Corner house at the junction of Heathland Road and St. Kilda's Road; one of several in the area.

LOCAL SHOPPING

Shakspeare Walk itself showing some of the better houses with their elegant and balanced proportions.

Shakspeare Walk

The large 3 storey terraced houses of Shakspeare Walk and Milton Grove along with the smaller late Victorian and early Edwardian houses of surrounding streets were declared a 'Housing Action Area' in 1976. The area has been the subject of much council concern since then and some environmental improvements have been made.

Allen Road contains the local shopping which is somewhat run down and the council plans to stimulate the area. Many of the houses are of very good quality with fine details like, for example, cornice work above the top storey windows. However, although there is some rehabilitation work going on, most of the houses are in need of improvement.

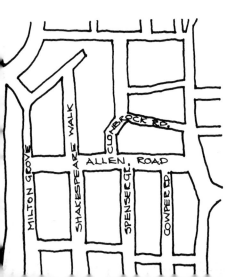

Some of the shops in Allen Road.

One of the several pubs in the area.

A view taken before the rehabilitation of the area began.

Broadway Market as restored, showing shops at ground level and houses above.

Broadway Market

The pocket of mostly neglected houses surrounds a surprisingly lively local shopping street remaining in an area which was once scheduled for redevelopment. Somehow it survived after all the plans that intended it to be demolished, and, because the climate of the times is now renovation rather than redevelopment, Broadway Market is now being successfully rehabilitated.

The charm of the area comes from the characterful shopping street and the tiny community around the shops and pubs. Numbers 75-81 Broadway Market are listed as buildings of historic importance but this fact has not prevented the severe neglect that the area has suffered.

Market scenes on a Saturday morning.

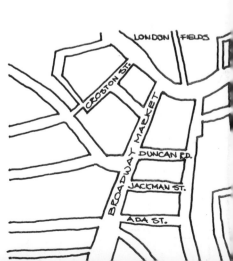

HOUSES NEXT TO PARKS

The majestic curve of the west part of Gore Road.

Gore Road

These 3 storey terraced houses are very regular and plain in their detail work. The classical columns and original windows are painted in light colours in contrast with the fine brickwork.

Contained in the curved terrace are a number of new houses, constructed on a bomb site, designed to fit in with the older houses. The elegant curve of the whole terrace faces Victoria Park, one of the landmarks of South Hackney.

House fronts showing the ground floor bay windows above basement bays. The plain columns and well recessed doors combined with the raised level give emphasis to the entrance.

The East end of Gore Road showing the new houses.

16

At the west end of Meynell Crescent these substantial houses have large bay windows.

The houses look directly on to the grass and trees of Well Street Common.

Meynell Crescent

The solid Victorian houses of this continuous terrace are built only on one side of the street so that the fronts of the houses face Well Street Common and contrast pleasantly with the green park. Their various details; classical porticos, upper storey bay windows with a splendid view, date plaques and plasterwork help this curving terrace to form a delightful composition.

To the east the houses are larger and more imposing with their entrances emphasised by columns.

17

THE HOUSE

Very few people own detached houses set apart from other buildings, and, the architecture associated with this kind of house is often very different from the architecture that is associated with Hackney. In Hackney most older houses are built in terraces that are part of a pattern of streets covering an area. They are not, however, monotonous terraces for in one terrace of houses there may be considerable variation in the details which give each house its own individuality.

Hopefully, some of the areas that have been looked at in the first section of this book have shown how houses in groups derive much of their character and appeal from their being part of a unified pattern.

There is a growing public awareness about conservation but many people feel that conservation is about special public buildings such as the Town Hall or a local church. Or, they feel that it is about Bloomsbury squares or Knightsbridge terraces. In fact, conservation is just as much about the Victorian houses of Hackney as it is about any other aspect of our heritage.

Most people think in terms of improving their houses at some point — putting in central heating, repainting windows, etc. — but they don't always think of the conservation aspects of keeping their property in good order. Alterations and general maintenance can be done badly and therefore detract from the overall character of the house and of the street, or, they can be done well, not only contributing to the overall harmony and balance of the street but also contributing to the beauty and value of the individual house.

A considerable amount of time and money has gone into emphasising this house with a smooth render finish. The house was very much a part of a composition which must be in harmony with the adjoining house. Applying colour has made the double house appear chopped in half and the regular rhythm of the street has been broken.

Good maintenance makes sound economic sense but it involves taking the time and trouble to be sensitive to the use of traditional materials and the effects of colour and texture. It also involves knowing something about older houses and it is hoped that this book will help people to learn more about their houses and feel confident that when they are doing repairs and alterations that they understand the consequences and effects of what they are doing. There is a section at the end of the book which will help with further information.

It cannot, however, be denied that conservation is also a matter of taste. There will always be aesthetic arguments about, for example, painting exterior brickwork. It is impossible simply to argue that the uncovered brickwork is better because that is what the Victorian builder intended the house to look like. Nevertheless, there are also sound practical and economic reasons for not painting brickwork and for

The rendered front of this small terraced house is applied without regard for the street as a whole. Removal of the band of plasterwork at roof level emphasises the loss of continuity.

retaining, repairing and replacing the original fabric of older houses.

It should be obvious that this book aims to show that if people really understand that their house is part of a unified pattern, part of

its surroundings, then they will aim to make the most of their houses as they are and not try to make them what they are not. A Victorian house was not designed to have large areas of glass; introducing picture windows destroys the balance of the composition in the facade. Painting the brickwork in a colour which must inevitably end abruptly at the neighbouring houses is to pretend that the house is detached from its surroundings when it is not. Removing facade details like plaques and cornices denudes the front of the house and removes its individuality within the group. Replacing slate roofing with orange concrete tiles makes a colour and texture break in the continuity of the street roofs.

Conservation must be the concern of the individual and not regarded as being in the hands of public authorities who do up' isolated buildings to give historic areas a facelift. What people do to their windows and doors in Hackney is just as important as what the Greater London Council does to old market buildings in Covent Garden.

This attempt to streamline Victorian houses by the removal of the original bay windows breaks up the pattern of pleasant repetition along the street and gives no real advantage to the individual house.

PARTS OF THE HOUSE
– Traditional Materials

Taking a good look at the individual house and the traditional materials used in building can really help towards understanding the merits of the original construction.

The Roof and Chimneys

Slate is the traditional material used for the roof covering. Although the material is basically smooth and grey there are subtle variations of colour and texture. Even the roof can have extra little details that add to the character of the house. Perhaps there are special ridge tiles that run along the street or iron-work 'finials' on roofing over upper storey bay windows, resembling weather vanes. Quite often each house has a different detail.

Chimneys make a punctuation point between houses. Clay pots can be of different design and heights.

External Walls

Walls are traditionally of brick. The colour is not 'flat' but little variations produce a rich, textured effect. Generally the bricks used in Hackney are London yellow stocks or sometimes Essex Reds. There are different 'bonds' (the way that the bricks are laid down on top of each other) and sometimes a combination of bonds are used in one house front. There may be brickwork arches over window and door openings of a special pattern of different coloured bricks making a continuous band along the street. Different styles of pointing and colours of mortar between the bricks produce different overall texture to the external wall.

Although brickwork is naturally porous it does not actually absorb much water because, as it ages, brickwork builds up a protective skin so that rainwater runs off. Any rainwater that is absorbed by the brick will evaporate quickly under normal conditions and brickwork need not give any problems with damp if the mortar is in good condition.

Sometimes a 'cornice' of plasterwork at the junction between wall and roof, rather like the plasterwork at ceiling level that may be in the front room, runs along the street binding it together. There may be other plasterwork details like date plaques or a plaque with the name of the house or a set of houses. Plasterwork around windows and doors is very common and emphasises the openings.

Windows

Windows are traditionally made of wood with parts that slide vertically on ropes that are an integral part of the window construction (called sash windows). The actual size of the panes of glass in the window and the different divisions was thought about in the original design of the house and is important to the proportion and balance of the facade.

The construction of traditional windows is such that parts can be replaced and sections of rotting timber can be mended. Unlike metal, wood is an easy material to work with.

Plasterwork surrounding window openings may have attractive designs or lintels and cills (the stone supports above and below the window) may have special mouldings. Plasterwork surrounds picked out with paintwork smoothly contrasting with the surrounding textured brickwork is characteristic of Victorian houses.

Bay windows are very common, either one at ground floor or continuing up to the first floor. There are a variety of details used like plasterwork columns with fruits and flowers moulded in the head of the column, or tiny upstands to ground floor bay windows resembling small balconies with decorations of leaves and flowers.

Doors

Doors are also traditionally of wood and sometimes have stained glass panels. Surrounds to doors with arches and columns emphasise the entrance and are usually built as one unit with the house next door. Heads to doorway columns are often very varied in one street, with moulded heads surrounded by leaves or bunches of grapes.

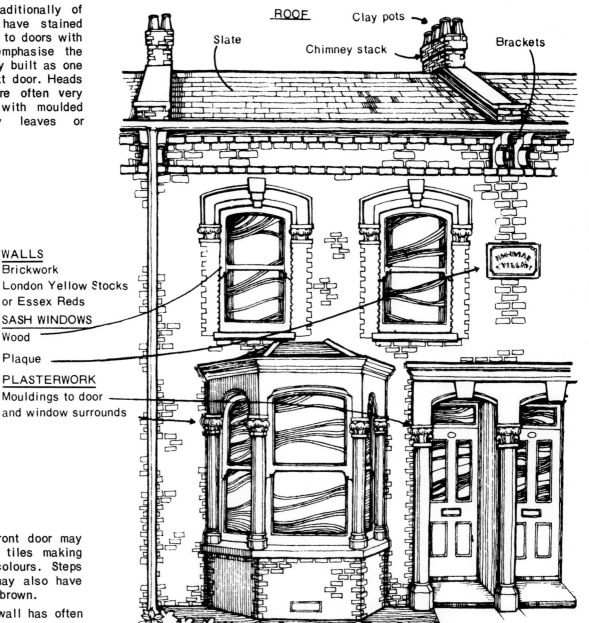

ROOF

Slate

Chimney stack

Clay pots

Brackets

WALLS
Brickwork
London Yellow Stocks
or Essex Reds
SASH WINDOWS
Wood

Plaque

PLASTERWORK
Mouldings to door
and window surrounds

Paths and Front Walls

The path to the front door may be of attractive small tiles making patterns in different colours. Steps up to the front door may also have tiles or be plain reddish brown.

The original front wall has often disappeared from older houses but occasionally there is some original ironwork or small brick walls with brick columns at the gateway. Small iron gates are characteristic.

THE ROOF

How the roof looks may not seem all that important when considering the overall appearance of the front of the house. However, as most 2 and 3 storey terrace houses have continuous roofing along the street which is clearly visible from the ground there is no reason why appearance should be neglected if reroofing is necessary.

The most obvious reason why the roof should be kept in good repair is that faulty roofs let in damp which causes decay and ruins decoration. If not treated, damp can lead to serious structural damage. Loose slates can be seen by looking up at the roof from the road or the back garden (a pair of binoculars helps) but it is a good idea to go into the loft during wet weather to check for leaks.

Roof repairs are essential and come before most other maintenance being considered. A builder should be called in if a problem is suspected and estimates are free. It is always a good idea to try and get a number of estimates if possible. Whereas one builder may feel it is necessary to completely reroof, another may feel able to patch up the existing roof material. It is possible that grants for carrying out repairs are available and people should get in touch with the local authority to find out what they may be eligible for. (see the last section of this book for further details).

If complete re-roofing is necessary and the price of new slate is considered too expensive then imitation slate of asbestos cement could be considered. From a distance it can look as good as the genuine article. Concrete tiles are much heavier than the slate which the roof timbers were originally designed to carry and the increased weight may be treble the weight of the old slate roof covering. It should be remembered that this may lead to sagging and the roof timbers may need to be strengthened. In extreme cases the additional weight can be sufficient to push the walls out if the roof is not strong enough. If it is thought that concrete tiles can be used then they can be obtained in grey to match the surrounding slate roofs and keep the continuity of the roof line.

For small renewal jobs, second-hand slates can be obtained. New slates can be bought singly or in quantity and all slates vary in size, shape and thickness. So, people who are attempting small repairs themselves will need to be sure that the new slate matches the old or complicated cutting will be necessary.

Concrete tiles next to finer and more varied texture of slate roof of neighbouring house appear clumsy. Details of ridge tiles and 'finial' have been removed from roofing over bay window. The chimney between the two houses has been repaired without thought for its appearance.

Chimneys are often neglected as they are so inaccessible. Sulphuric acid from smoke and damp can eat away mortar. Loose bricks, damaged flaunching (the sloped mortar fillet around the chimney pot), defective flashing (the weatherproof seal used where the roof abuts a chimney stack) and broken pots can all be repaired or replaced. Repairs should be done with materials to match.

A chimney that is not being used can be capped off with a ventilation 'spigot' which allows air to circulate. There is no need to remove a chimney that is not in use and repairs may be cheaper and leave the option of using coal in the future. Coal is going to be around longer than oil or gas and in these days of uncertainty over sources of fuel it makes no sense to remove a chimney which may be important in the future.

Removal of roofing over this bay window and its replacement with a flat roof breaks up the roof pattern of the street.

Dormer window facing the street looks unbalanced.

Alterations to extend the roof space will affect the appearance of the house from the street. If dormer windows are being put in then it is more sensible to make them face the garden side of the house which will be quieter and not affect the appearance of the front. 'Off-the-peg' glazed roof lights will be cheaper than dormer windows and can be used for rooms facing the front.

WALLS

The solid brickwork walls of older houses were usually constructed by skilled bricklayers using good quality bricks. There is no reason why, with some sensible maintenance, brickwork walls should not continue to exclude the weather and look good at the same time.

The most important maintenance to be carried out is repointing. This means that the mortar joints between the bricks are raked out and replaced with new mortar. The joints may be flush with the brick forming a flat surface, or they may be slightly sloped or 'weather struck' to give maximum protection from damp. It may be that only one section of the wall needs repointing in which case the old joints must match the new and the mortar be colour-matched with the old. Once repointing has been done it is unlikely that the brickwork will need any attention for many years.

Damaged bricks can be replaced with a new brick that has been cut in half along its length and inserted where the crumbling parts of the old brick have been chipped out. Whole bricks can be removed one by one if necessary (the wall won't fall down) but it is important that in all cases the new bricks match the old. Generally second-hand London yellow stocks will blend in with most buildings.

If there are additional problems with damp, like for example rising damp, then the cause must be traced. If the external wall is simply coated with paint or render before the damp problem has been properly tackled then serious problems may result.

Damp proof courses do exist in older houses but new chemical D.P.C.s

This mixture of painted brickwork and render cuts this house off from the neighbouring houses of untreated brickwork. Perhaps the owner intended to show individuality; the house is certainly different but how is it better?

can be installed to prevent rising damp from the ground. This is relatively inexpensive if the problem is tackled early in its development, but, if the internal plaster gets wet then the problem will be a lot more serious. This kind of work must be done by experts.

Junctions between the wall and window timbers can sometimes be a cause of damp penetration if the wood has shrunk away from the wall. Water staining on the brickwork around the window area is evidence that this is happening or it may be that the cill is faulty (see later).

Damaged gutters and drainpipes can direct water at the wall and cause damp penetration. It is an easy matter to check whether this is happening and renew defective guttering etc.

This newly painted house has an unreal cartoon-like character which stops dead at the junction between the two houses.

This kind of flaking is common in painted brickwork. It will be difficult to patch up one corner; probably the house will have to be expensively repainted.

Painting or rendering is absolutely useless if all the above work has not been done first. If rendering or painting is not done properly it is likely that a lot of trouble may be caused unnecessarily. Brickwork can rot under gloss paint. Paint that is applied without following the makers instructions exactly can flake quickly and in any case will need renewal after about 4 years. Rendering can crack badly and look very unsightly and if small pockets of air are caught between the render and the brickwork they can hold water and damp will get into the house. Quite simply, additional coatings to brickwork are unnecessary and expensive.

From the appearance point of view, covering up brickwork is going to break up the street rhythm and make the individual house look out of step in the terrace. Render and paint work often only cover up the individuality and charm of the house and they have no real practical advantage.

WINDOWS

Timber windows that have not been looked after may start jamming, the frames may warp causing the glass to crack or become loose and joints can rot or break. A good do-it-yourself manual will show how to tackle all of these problems. It may be that the frame has to be dismantled and some parts replaced, or damaged sections be cut out and replaced.

However, it is important to bear in mind that the window in question may have already lasted for 100 years and suffered a lot of neglect. It is not necessary to think first of replacement. This solution may apparently be the easiest but it is unlikely to be the cheapest. The windows were designed to last and made with well matured timber. Window frames that are regularly painted for protection will last a very long time.

If new windows really are necessary then a replacement window of the original type will fit the opening that is already there. This is the simplest and most economical solution. New window types may involve altering the size of the opening which involves extra cost and can have structural implications. Many people carry out extensive building work in order to put in new window types such as aluminium which may have no real advantages over the window type that existed before. Properly fitting wood window frames work smoothly, are designed to let in sufficient light according to the size of of the rooms and look good as a part of the original design of the house.

This new bay window has no advantage over the original; it gives no extra space or light and lacks character.

26

A badly proportioned new window that destroys the balance that existed in the original house.

Removal of the bay window flattens the front of the house, reduces the size of the front room and cuts out light.

The size and numbers of existing window panes are intended to be a part of the balance and order of the house front; alterations to this existing balance are not always damaging but care must be taken. Louvres seem to be a favourite small alteration which can look very fussy and the fixed glass below is difficult to clean, especially if it is a first floor window. Ventilation in summer is not sufficient and well fitted timber windows are just as efficient, in winter, to stop draughts.

Paint fulfils a vital role in protecting timber. Flaking and chipped paint looks unpleasant and allows the wood to absorb moisture and swell up. Light painted window frames always look good next to traditional brickwork, contrasting well with the darker texture finish of the bricks. If the window surrounds are painted in a pale colour this helps more light to get into the rooms.

Patchy brickwork due to removal of original windows - new window size has no advantage over the old.

DOORS

Solid timber doors to older houses are constructed of well seasoned wood of fine quality (unavailable nowadays). They only need to be painted to keep them in good order. Older doors are generally much wider and taller than modern doors so replacing the old door with a flush timber one or clouded glass type may not be as easy as it seems. It will probably have to be specially made to fit.

The original door was made as a part of the design of the house. Doors along the street will match in type and size but may be painted in many different colours. Maybe it doesn't seem all that important to worry about what kind of door a house had — perhaps the photographs on this page are the best way to show the different impressions that different doors give. However, it is worth remembering that most people who call round to see each other spend a minute standing looking at the front door before it's opened!

DETAILS

Traditional details to Victorian house fronts are very varied and often a mark of the individuality of each house. Some details, like a continuous band of plasterwork above the upper storey windows, bind the terrace together. Other details may be barge boards, finials, entrance porches and canopies.

When details are removed, which is very common when people attempt to 'modernise' their houses the facade can appear very bleak. Date plaques, plasterwork etc. will leave unsightly marks on the brickwork if they are removed. Some builders may even advise removing them (really because they cannot be bothered with small work). However, there is no reason why they should be removed and it makes sense to get another more skilled builder to look at the work if the first builder is unwilling to do the work.

Attention to these details is very much a question of taking extra time and trouble to think in terms of small repairs and not to immediately opt for the apparently easy, but sometimes costly, solution of removing detail work. The house can benefit equally from protecting internal details like mouldings fireplaces, original doors, etc.

Expensive 'improvements' to this house have left it characterless and bare. Almost all the detail work has been removed except plasterwork above the door. The importance of this detail as an emphasis to the entrance is lost because it is painted the same colour as the walls.

To attach a metal plate above the door, detail work has been removed and leaving an unsightly mark.

It is a good idea to take a look at houses around Hackney which have been sensitively treated and make comparisons with those that have not. It soon becomes clear that the better looking houses are those that try to retain the details which are an integral part of the original design.

The photographs on this page show some of the many varied and interesting details which can be found in Hackney.

Column head and base unhappily divided into two by different paintwork.

A Note on Energy Conservation

A Note on Energy Conservation

Energy saving measures are now becoming an important part of home maintenance. Many of the ways of reducing fuel bills require alterations which affect the appearance of the house. Expensive measures like double glazing, wall insulation fixed to internal walls and rendering to outside walls are the sorts of elaborate solutions that the building industry wants to sell people. The kind of work that needs to be done is often very simple and need not be expensive. The extra comfort will be immediately felt and within a couple of years any initial spending will be offset by the money saved in fuel bills.

Where the heat goes (energy losses)

30%   of the heat in an average house is lost in ventilation. Not only an open window or door is to blame but also cracks around window frames and in the frame itself.

30%   leaks through the roof of the house.

30%   disappears through the walls. This percentage is even higher if parts of the wall are damp.

10%   of the heat is lost through the floor.

How to reduce heat losses

— Become energy conscious. The fuel bill will depend very much on the personal habits of people living in the house. How often doors and windows are left open and for how long will have much more effect on fuel consumption than whether there is single or double glazing in the house.

— Reduce ventilation losses by thorough draught stripping to windows and doors. Window frames should be repaired and cracks filled in around the frames (see section on windows).

— People who have central heating are often using one or two rooms but the whole house is being heated to a high temperature. Automatic thermostats on each radiator will lower the average air temperature and save energy costs by up to 10% per degree centigrade lowered.

— Insulation measures can often be very simple. Heavy curtains or shutters used at night can cut out some of the cold and a curtain over the front door can do the same. Loft insulation can be done with the aid of a grant (see the last section of this book) and it will cost less if home owners do it themselves.

These are a few of the measures that should be considered. There are various books available that give more details on this subject some of which can be found in the book list at the back of this book.

WHO CAN HELP
Local Government Organisations

Director of Planning and Development
Planning Division
Directorate of Planning
& Development,
161-189 City Road,
London, EC1V 1JL
Tel: 253 8455

The Planning Division can give information as to whether properties are in Conservation Areas, Housing Action Areas and General Improvement Areas or if the property is a listed building. This affects the amount and type of grants available and, in the case of historic buildings, the type of work that can be undertaken. For all properties certain kinds of alterations and extensions need planning permission. Always check with the Planning Department before doing any work.

The District Surveyor

London Borough of Hackney
23/25 Sutton Place
E9 6EH
Tel. 986 5314

Most matters relating to building control are dealt with at this office. It is very important to consult the District Surveyor when carrying out work, even if it is very small.

Building by-laws approval may be necessary, in the same way as planning permission, for structural alterations. Always check before carrying out any work including any matters relating to drainage and sewage (e.g. putting in a new bathroom or toilet), lighting and ventilation in certain cases.

Directorate of Technical Services
Environmental Health Division
205 Morning Lane E8
Tel. 986 3266

Following re-organisation, this office now has a very limited role in building works and the first call should be to the District Surveyor. Queries relating to actual living conditions will still be dealt with by the Environmental Health Office.

Directorate of Housing
Comprehensive Housing Service
287 Mare Street (next to the Town Hall)
E8 1EB
Tel. 986 3191

The 'Improvement Unit' of the Comprehensive Housing Service will give information about house renovation grants and explain what grants are available for particular properties. They can send a surveyor from the Advice Core of the Directorate of Housing to look at the property and advise on the work that is required. The service is free. The improvement Unit will give information to the Legal Advice Department which is situated on the ground floor of the Town Hall. They deal with the actual application for house renovation grant and can be contacted at the telephone number above.

Hackney Housing Centre
302/4 Mare Street
E8 1HA
Tel. 986 3123

This is the best place to start with if you want general information. The Housing Centre exists mainly to provide information for council tenants but they also have a comprehensive display of free leaflets about improvement grants, planning permission, compulsory purchase etc. They also advise on house purchase and have lists of houses for sale in the area. They will be able to refer you to other sections of the Local Authority Administration if they cannot help themselves.

WHO CAN HELP
Organisations

The Federation of Master Builders
33 John Street, WC1
Tel: 242 7583

The Federation has a list of builders who are registered with them. They can provide a list of builders who are approved by them in any area.

This does not mean that the work will be guaranteed but people having problems with a builder can make complaints to the organisation. They have started a list of 'warranted' builders and they hope that within the next year they will be able to provide a guarantee for alteration work.

Institute of Plumbers
Scottish Mutual House
North Street, Hornchurch
Essex RM11 1RU
Tel: 04024 72791

Anyone can call themselves a plumber but a 'qualified' plumber will most likely be registered by the Institute. This is not a guarantee of the work but at least it is a guarantee that the plumber is qualified to carry out the work.

Confederation for the Registration of Gas Installers (CORGI)
57a New Broadway, W5
Tel: 840 0046

Qualified gas installers will be registered with the confederation and must comply with gas safety regulations. As before, registration is a recommendation, not a guarantee. Complaints can be taken to the Confederation.

National Inspection Council for Electrical Contractors
Vintage House
36 Albert Embankment, SE1
Tel: 582 7746

As with the Plumbers, a registered Electrician carries some kind of recommendation but not a guarantee. The Inspection Council will listen to complaints about their members and inspect their work if requested.

The Building Centre
26 Store Street, WC1
Tel: General Enquiries 0344 884999
Administration 637 1022

The Building bookshop at the centre has an excellent range or technical and non-technical books and magazines relating to all aspects of building and do-it-yourself. They also have free leaflets and samples of building materials as well as exhibitions and general information.

Royal Institute of British Architects
66 Portland Place
Tel: 580 5533

If undertaking new building work or extensions and alterations it may be necessary to use an architect. For a list of architects in the area consult the R.I.B.A. For a list of chartered building surveyors consult the Royal Institute of Chartered Surveyors (R.I.C.S).

OTHER USEFUL ADDRESSES

The Civic Trust
17 Carlton House Terrace, SW1
Tel: 930 0914

The Victorian Society
1 Priory Gardens, W4
Tel: 994 1019

Centerprise Bookshop Community Project
136 Kingsland High Street, E8
Tel: 254 9632

The Georgian Group
37 Spital Square, E1
Tel: 377 1822

Society for the Protection of Ancient Buildings (SPAB)
37 Spital Square, E1
Tel: 377 1644

The London Architectural Salvage and Supply Co. Ltd. (LASCO)
Mark Street, E2
Tel: 739 0448/9

BOOKS

ABOUT HACKNEY

HACKNEY SOCIETY PUBLICATIONS
From Tower to Tower Block
The Victorian Villas of Hackney
South Shoreditch — Historic and Industrial Buildings

CENTERPRISE PUBLICATIONS
A Second Look
A Hackney Camera 1883-1918

HOME MAINTENANCE

The Readers' Digest Complete Home Maintenance
Published by the Readers' Digest
Looking after your House Basic guides published as
small leaflets by the Readers' Digest
Self-Help Repairs Manual A. Ingham — Penguin 1975
The Sunday Times Do-it-Yourself The Sunday Times
— Sphere Paperbacks 1976
The Reluctant Handyman Patrick Keegan and Ian
Layzell — Macmillan Papermac 1981

CONSERVATION

How to Restore and Improve your Victorian House
Alan Johnson — David and Charles 1984
*Putting Back the Style: A Directory of Authentic
Renovation* Ed. Alexandra Artley — Evans 1982
The House Restorer's Guide Hugh Lander — David
and Charles 1986
Your Hourse — the outside view John Prizeman —
Hutchinson 1975

DEPARTMENT OF THE ENVIRONMENT LEAFLETS
Available from the D.O.E., Her Majesty's Stationery
Office and The Housing Centre.

Home Improvement Grants
Planning Permission — a guide for householders
All about Loft, Tank and Pipe Insulation
Insulation against Traffic Noise
Your Home and Compulsory Purchase
Housing Defects

ENERGY

Keeping Warm for Half the Cost — the complete guide to home insulation Phil Townsend and John Colesby — Prism Press 1981
Beginners Guide to Home Energy Peter Campbell — Newnes Technical Books 1980

SPAB TECHNICAL PAMPHLETS

Outward Leaning Walls	Order No. 14/1
Strengthening Timber Floors	14/2
Chimneys in Old Buildings	14/3
Cleaning of Stone and Brick	14/4
Pointing of Stone and Brick Walling	14/5
Fire Safety in Historic Buildings	14/6
Treatment of Damp in Old Buildings	14/8
Electrical Wiring in Old Buildings	14/9

Each pamphlet costs £1 per copy, plus 20p p&p each.

For the many other SPAB publications, contact the Society.

BUILDING CENTRE LEAFLETS

Available from the Information Counter in the basement.

Thermal Insulation for Solid Walls	20p
Sound in the Home	30p
Condensation	20p
Wood	30p
Cavity Wall Insulation	20p
Loft/Roof Insulation	20p
Draught-proofing and Ventilation	30p
Domestic Space and Water Heating Controls	30p
Installing Domestic Space and Water Heating Systems	30p
Special Needs Housing	30p
Dampness in Buildings	30p

Postage and packing charge:
One to three fact sheets — 20p
Four to eleven fact sheets — 30p

The Hackney Society

The Hackney Society was founded in 1968 to encourage by all possible means the improvement of the environment of the London Borough of Hackney, its buildings, streets and open spaces. The Society has attracted most publicity over the years as a watchdog for local buildings of historic or visual importance. But it is equally concerned about broader issues in the treatment of the environment like the use of land, the enhancement of open space and the quality of new buildings erected by public authorities in the area. Broadly speaking, we are interested in any means of making Hackney a pleasanter place in which to live and work.

Membership Secretary:
Marilyn Douglas-Hamilton,
7 Stamford Grove West,
London N16
01-806 6075

For further information about the Society contact the Chairman:

David Batchelder,
16 Meynell Gardens, London E9.
01-985 7937